POWERING CARS

Nicolas Brasch

NELSON
CENGAGE Learning

Australia • Brazil • Japan • Korea • Mexico • Singapore • Spain • United Kingdom • United States

Powering Cars

Fast Forward
Green Level 14

Text: Nicolas Brasch
Editor: Johanna Rohan
Design: Vonda Pestana
Series design: James Lowe
Production controller: Emma Hayes
Photo research: Corrina Tauschke
Audio recordings: Juliet Hill, Picture Start
Spoken by: Matthew King and Abbe Holmes
Reprint: Siew Han Ong

Acknowledgements
The author and publisher would like to acknowledge permission to reproduce material from the following sources: Photographs by AAP Image/Bikas Das, p 15; APL/Corbis/Reuter Raymond, p 17/ Chaiwat Subprasom, p 19; Getty Images/Peter Dazeley, back cover, pp 3, 22/ Mustafa Ozer, pp 20, 21, 23/ RF, p 11/ Stockbyte, p 5 top; Istockphoto.com/Clayton Hansen, p 16; James Ward, cover, p 1; Lonely Planet Images/Michael Aw, p 4/ Dennis Johnson, p 13; Newsphotos.com/ Stephen Laffer, p 18; Newspix.com.au, p 7; Photolibrary.com/Warwick Kent, p 4 inset/ Graham Monro, p 10/ SUPERSTOCK, p 8/ Werner Thomas, p 5 bottom/ Photolibrary.com/Age Fotostock/Manfred Bauman, p 6/ Regis Martin, p 12; Photos.com, p 9; Science & Society Picture Library/Science Museum, p 14.

ISBN 978 0 17 012593 2
ISBN 978 0 17 012585 7 (set)

Cengage Learning Australia
Level 7, 80 Dorcas Street
South Melbourne, Victoria Australia 3205
Phone: 1300 790 853

Cengage Learning New Zealand
Unit 4B Rosedale Office Park
331 Rosedale Road, Albany, North Shore NZ 0632
Phone: 0508 635 766

For learning solutions, visit cengage.com.au

Printed in Australia by Ligare Pty Ltd
7 8 9 10 11 12 13 20 19 18 17 16

THE UNIVERSITY OF MELBOURNE

Evaluated in independent research by staff from the Department of Language, Literacy and Arts Education at the University of Melbourne.

POWERING CARS

Nicolas Brasch

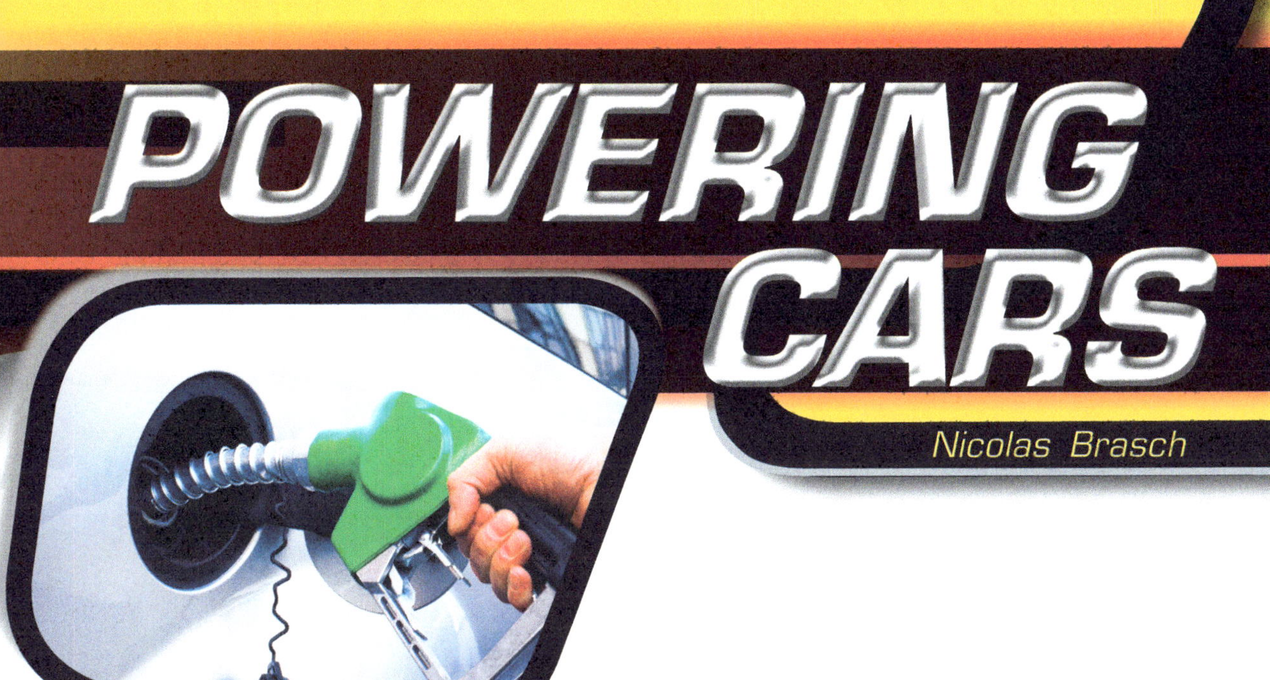

Contents

Chapter 1

CARS IN SOCIETY

Every day, thousands of cars are driven around the world.

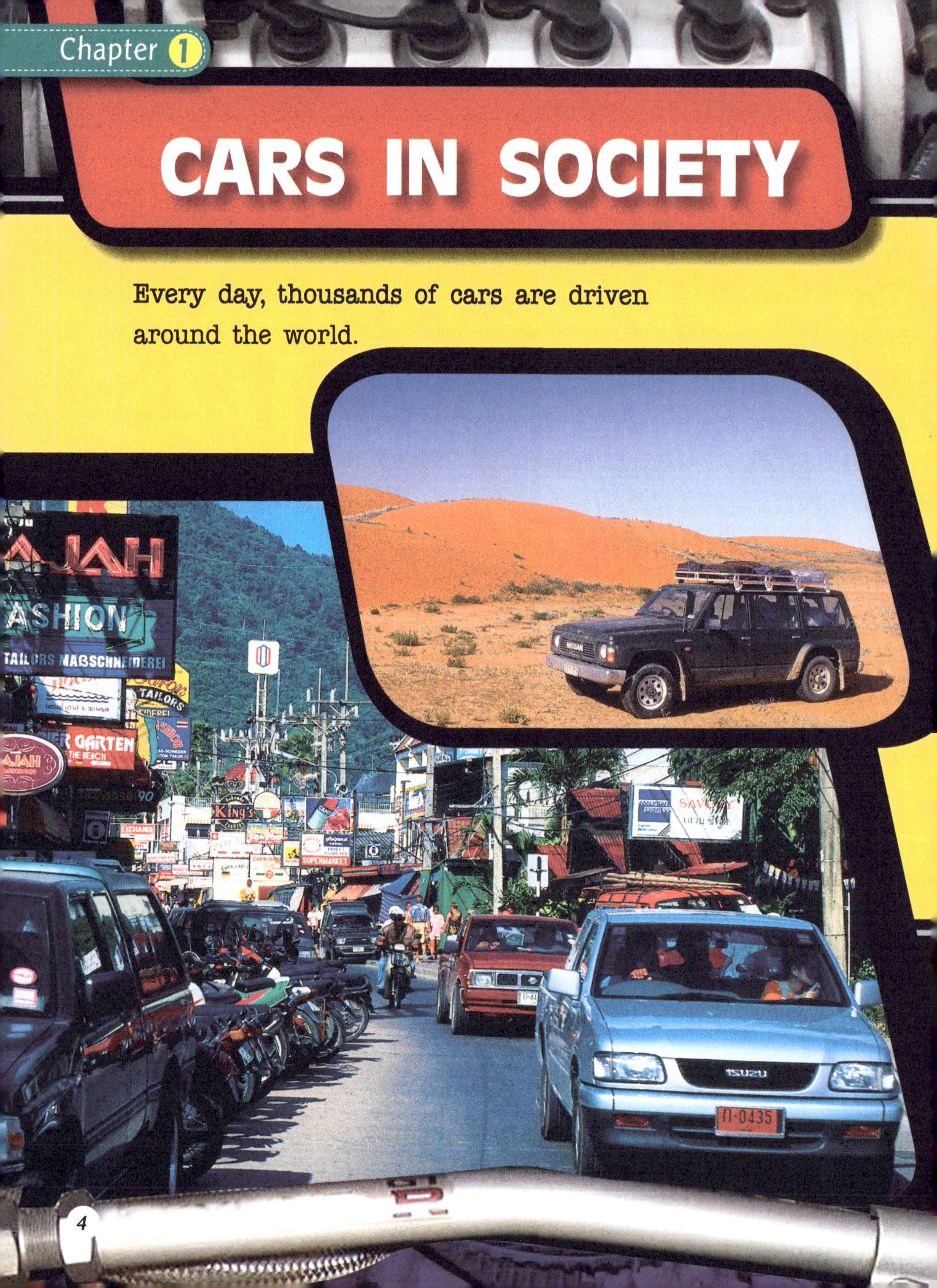

Cars take people to school and work. They have become an important part of everyday life.

Most cars are powered by petrol.
But there are other ways to power cars.

Cars can also run on gas and **electricity**.

What are the pros and cons of petrol, gas and electricity?

Chapter 2

WHY PETROL IS GOOD

Petrol is a form of energy used to power cars. It comes from petroleum, which is mined from under the ground or the sea.

a petroleum mine at sea

It is quite easy to get the petroleum from under the ground or sea. Mining companies can get a lot of petroleum at one time.

It is also quite easy to make petrol from petroleum.

Petrol is easy to transport,
store and handle.
It can be transported safely to a petrol station
in a truck.

Running Words 161

Then, it can be pumped easily
into the petrol storage tanks.
Finally, it can be pumped from the storage tanks
into the car.

Chapter 3

WHY PETROL IS BAD

Not everything about petrol is good. Petrol gives off **carbon dioxide**, which is bad for the environment.

Carbon dioxide is a gas.
When petrol is burnt,
it gives off carbon dioxide.
This harms the Earth's **atmosphere**.

Some petrol has **lead** added to it.
This improves the petrol's performance.

Lead is a metal.
When lead is burnt,
it can cause health problems
for many people.

Chapter 4

USING GAS TO POWER CARS

Gas is an alternative to petrol. One type of gas that is used to power cars is called Liquid Petroleum Gas or **LPG**.

an LPG bottle

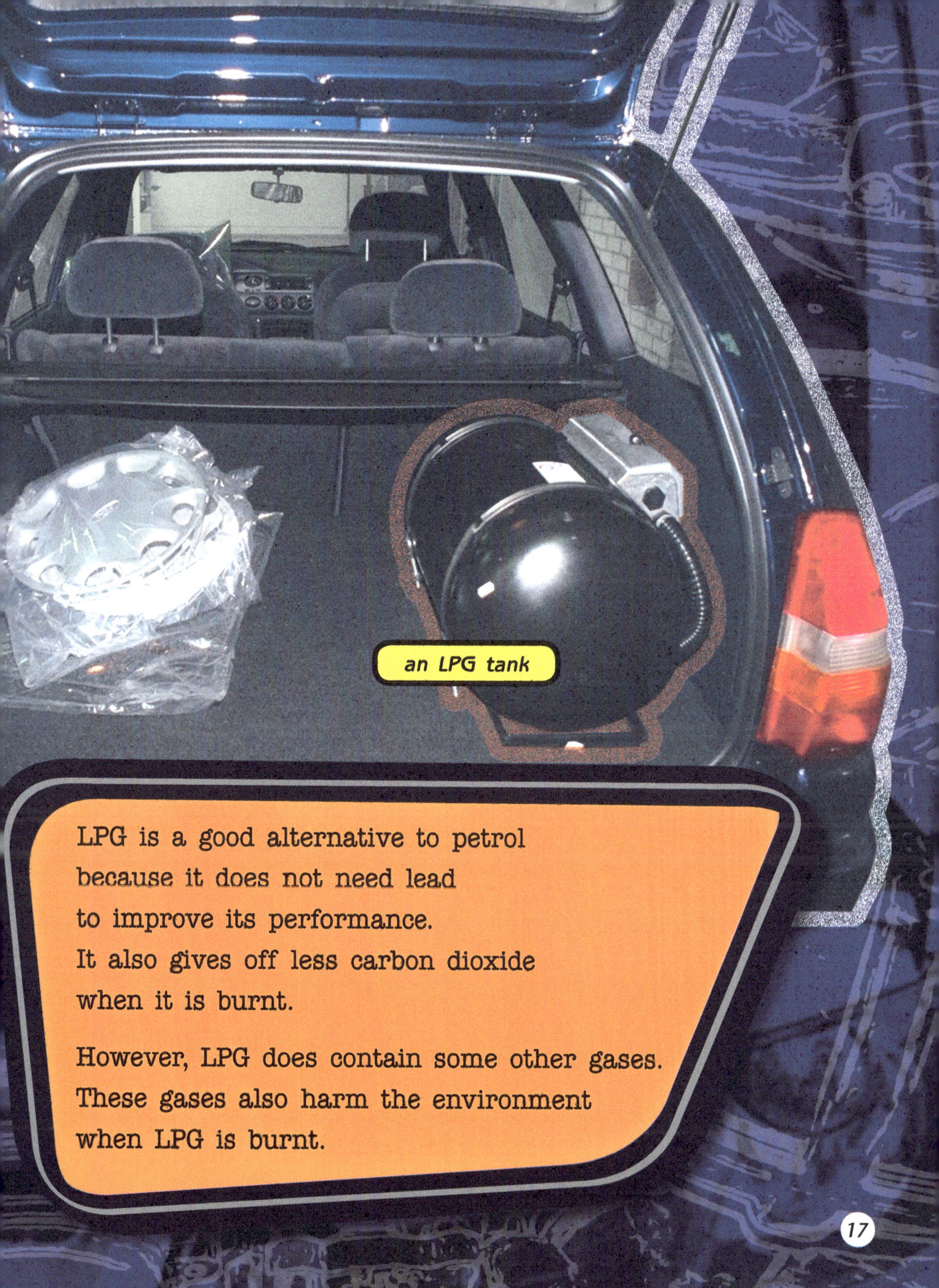

LPG is a good alternative to petrol because it does not need lead to improve its performance. It also gives off less carbon dioxide when it is burnt.

However, LPG does contain some other gases. These gases also harm the environment when LPG is burnt.

While it is quite cheap to produce LPG, car owners still have to pay a lot of money to power their cars with LPG. This is because most cars are made to run on petrol.

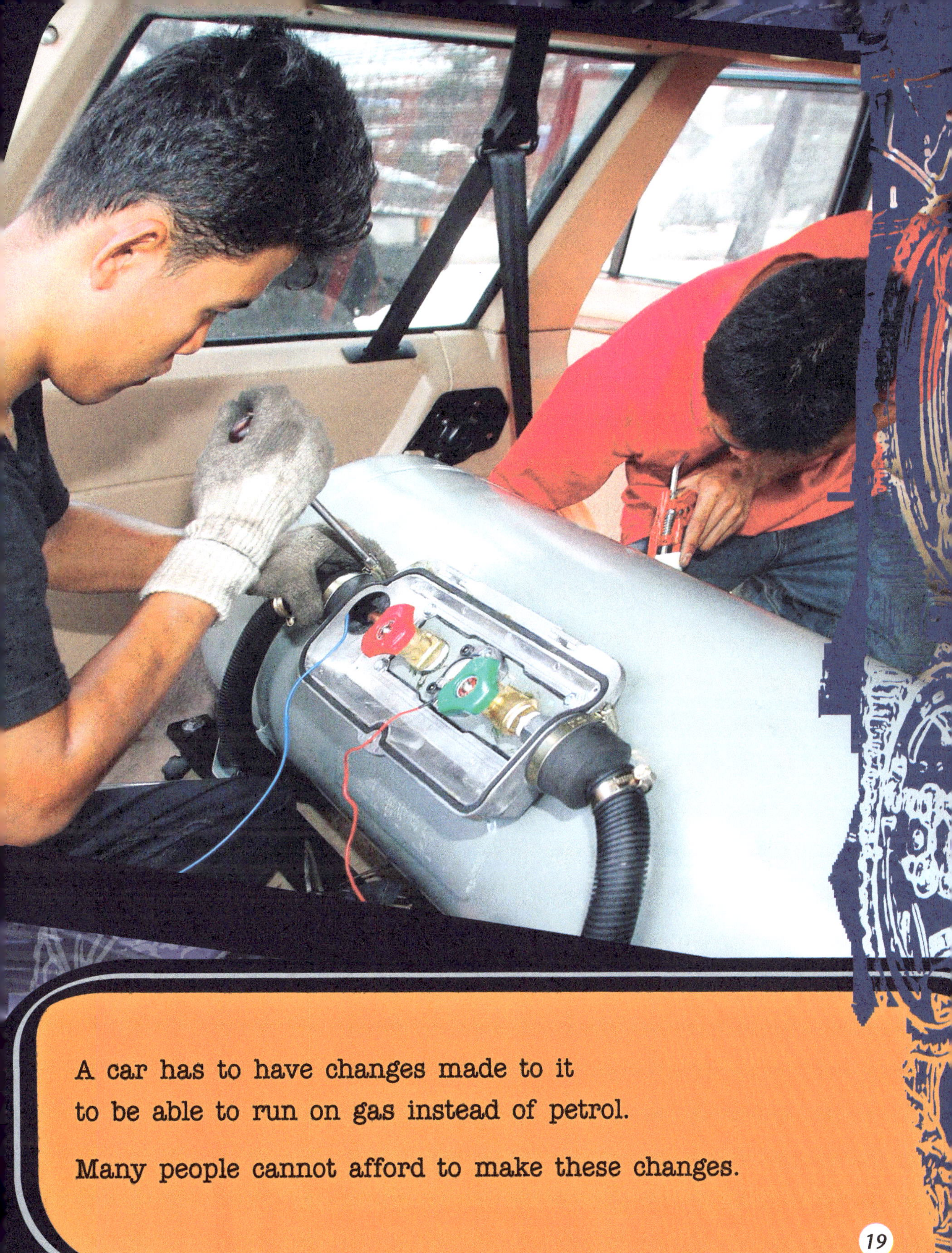

A car has to have changes made to it to be able to run on gas instead of petrol.

Many people cannot afford to make these changes.

Chapter 5

USING ELECTRICITY TO POWER CARS

Electricity is another alternative to petrol.

Electricity can be stored in a battery that is fitted to the car. Sometimes, the electricity is produced by **solar power**.

Solar power is power that comes from the heat and light of the Sun.

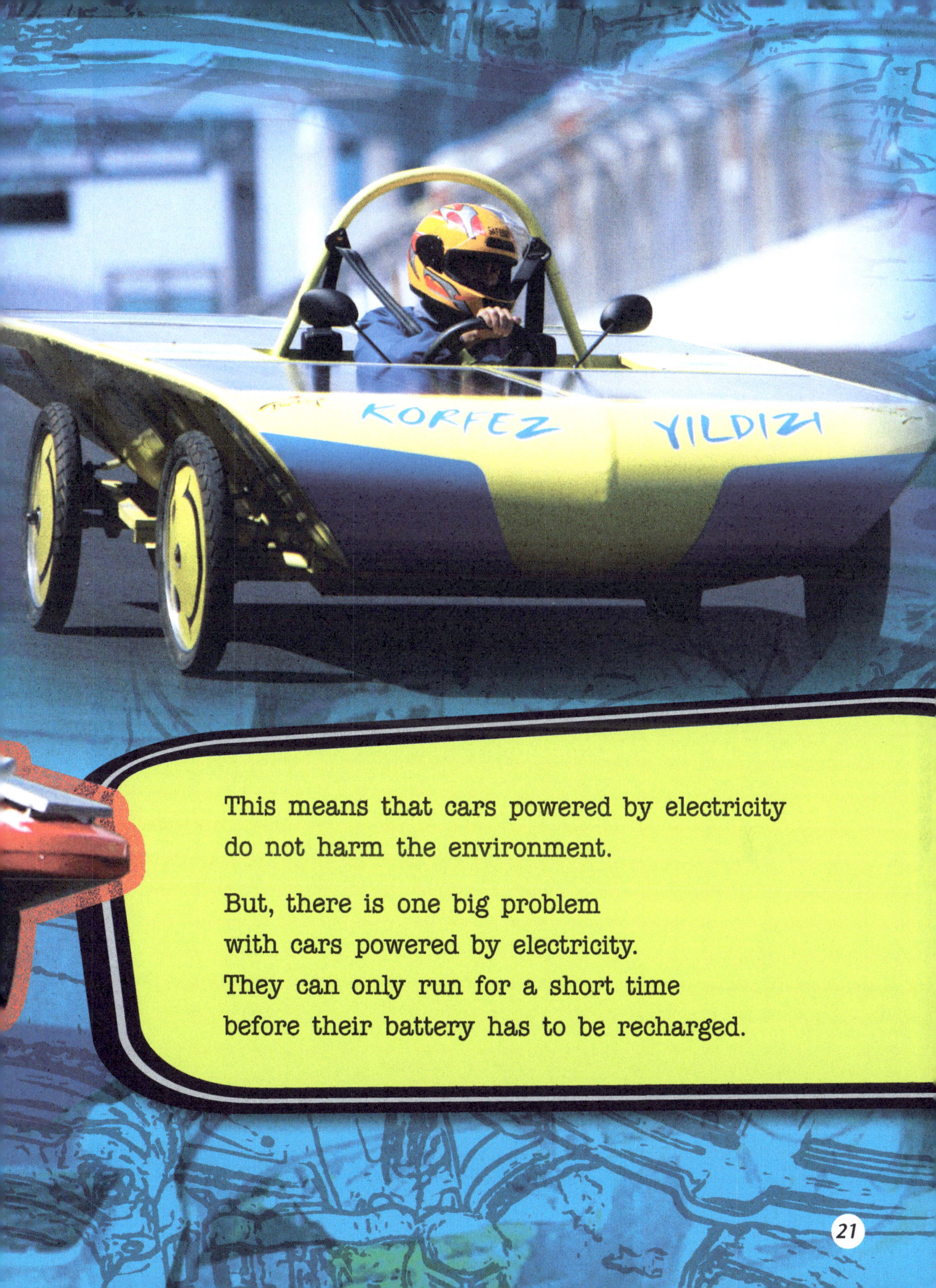

This means that cars powered by electricity do not harm the environment.

But, there is one big problem with cars powered by electricity. They can only run for a short time before their battery has to be recharged.

Chapter 6

PROS AND CONS

Petrol

Pros

- cheap to use
- easy to store
- easy to transport
- easy to handle

Cons

- bad for the environment
- bad for people's health

Gas

Pros

- does not need lead to improve its performance
- gives off less carbon dioxide when burnt than petrol

Cons

- cars need to be changed to run on gas
- this change costs a lot of money

Electricity

Pros

- not bad for the environment
- power can come from the Sun

Cons

- cars cannot run for very long without recharging their battery

Glossary

atmosphere	the layer of gases surrounding the Earth
carbon dioxide	a colourless, odourless gas
electricity	a form of energy
lead	a heavy metal
LPG	Liquid Petroleum Gas. A gas made from petroleum.
solar power	power made by using the energy from the Sun

Index